CZERNY-SCHAUM

The Purpose of the Czerny-Schaum Edition

Carl Czerny (1791–1857) was a prolific composer who wrote approximately 1,000 published compositions. As a pupil of Beethoven and the teacher of Liszt, he was a transmitter of ideas from one great master to another. Czerny began his distinguished career as a piano teacher at the age of 15. As well as Beethoven's nephew Karl, other famous pupils included Kullak and Heller. His many collections of exercises and studies range from the easy and progressive to the virtuoso. The Czerny-Schaum edition is based on selections from Op. 599, Op. 139, Op. 821, Op. 718, Op. 636, and Op. 261. The objective is to bring together, in condensed form, excerpts that stress many varieties of technical problems. Special emphasis is placed on equal development of both hands. The technical points are equally divided between the right and the left hands. The exercises are purposely brief, thereby avoiding stiffness and tension. Using the Czerny-Schaum exercises will improve piano technic when used in conjunction with a program of balanced piano repertoire.

Editor: Gail Lew
Production Coordinator: Sharon Marlow
Cover Illustration: Magdi Rodríguez
Cover Design: María A. Chenique

Contents

Five-Finger Legato (right hand) 3

Five-Finger Legato (left hand) 3

Right-Hand Legato 4

Left-Hand Legato 4

Melodic Phrasing 5

Broken Thirds (right hand) 6

Broken Thirds (left hand) 6

Alternating Legato and Staccato 7

Forearm Rotation 7

Scale Patterns (both hands) 8

Right-Hand Trill Study 9

Left-Hand Trill Study 9

Scale Passages (right hand) 10

Scale Passages (left hand) 10

Left-Hand Melody Playing 11

Broken Chords (right hand) 12

Broken Chords (left hand) 12

Wrist Staccato (right hand) 13

Wrist Staccato (left hand) 14

Left-Hand Legato Study 14

Melody Study in Thirds 15

Repeated Notes 16

Accompaniment Pattern (left hand) 16

Right-Hand Turn Technic 17

Left-Hand Turn Technic 17

Study in Phrasing 18

Chromatic Contractions (right hand) 19

Chromatic Contractions (left hand) 19

Chord Inversions 20

Interweaving Hand Legato 20

Broken Chords (divided hands) 21

Legato and Staccato 22

Crossing Hands Study 22

Triplet Study 23

Accompaniment Design 23

Continuous Scale Passages 24

Holding Top Notes (right hand) 25

Holding Bottom Notes (right hand) 25

Holding Top Notes (left hand) 26

Holding Bottom Notes (left hand) 26

Accompaniment in Triplets 27

Two-Note Slurs 28

Strengthening Fingers 4 and 5 29

Accompaniment Patterns
(with finger extensions) 29

Accompaniment in Thirds 30

Velocity in Five-Finger Groups (right hand) ... 31

Velocity in Five-Finger Groups (left hand) 31

Left-Hand Staccato Melody 32

FIVE-FINGER LEGATO

right hand

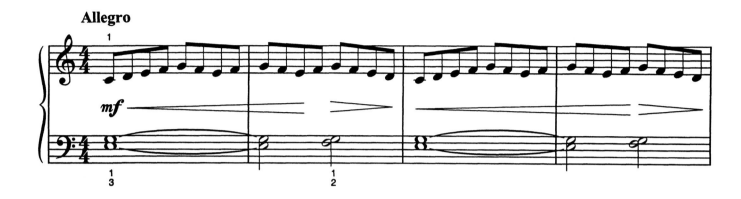

FIVE-FINGER LEGATO

left hand

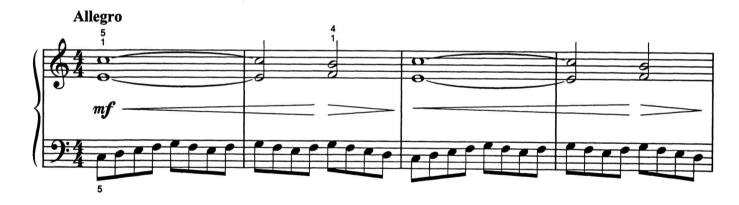

EL00285A

RIGHT-HAND LEGATO

Allegro moderato

LEFT-HAND LEGATO

Allegro moderato

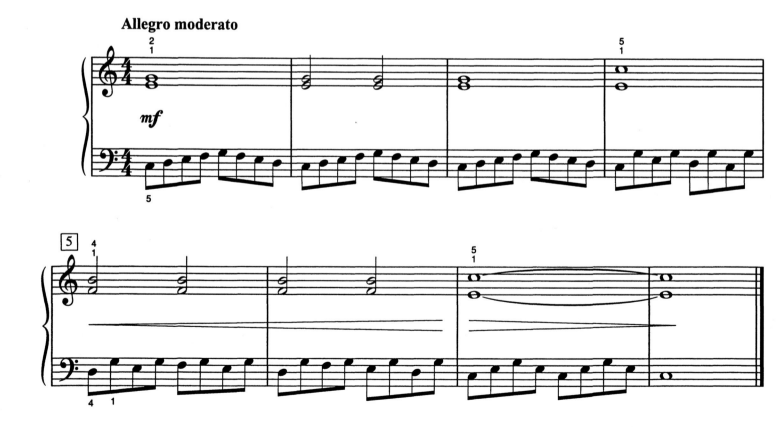

MELODIC PHRASING

BROKEN THIRDS
right hand

BROKEN THIRDS
left hand

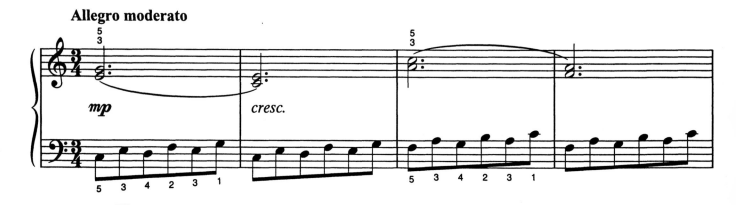

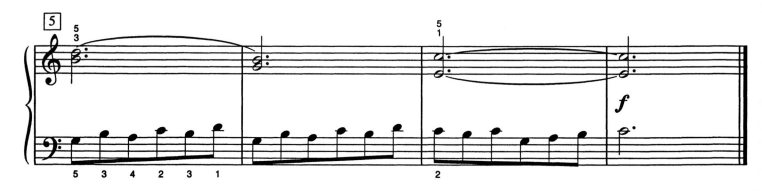

ALTERNATING LEGATO
AND STACCATO

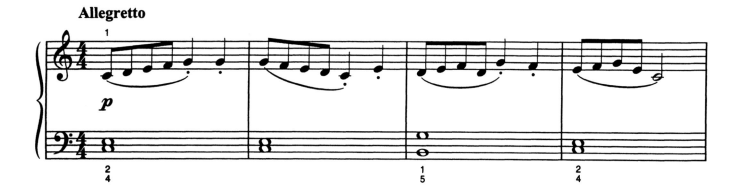

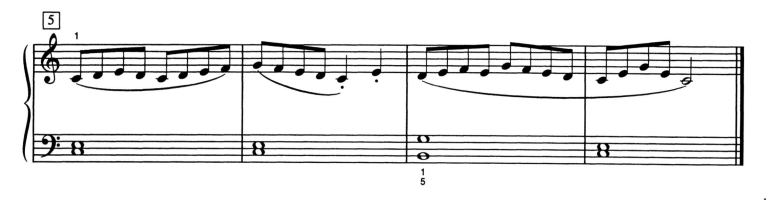

FOREARM ROTATION

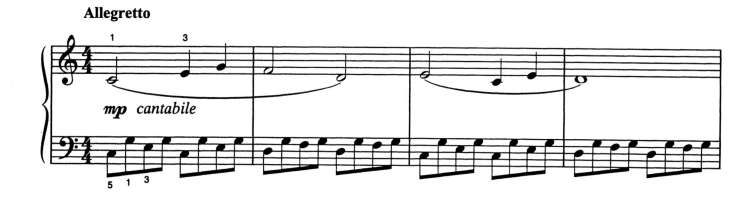

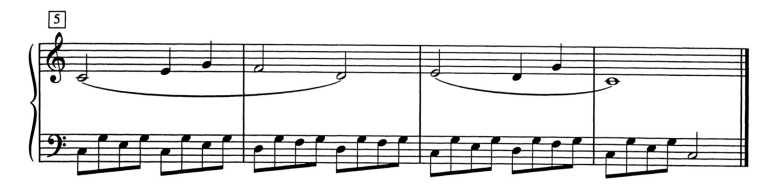

EL00285A

SCALE PATTERNS
both hands

RIGHT-HAND TRILL STUDY

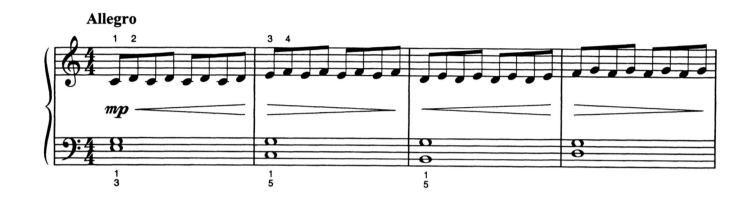

LEFT-HAND TRILL STUDY

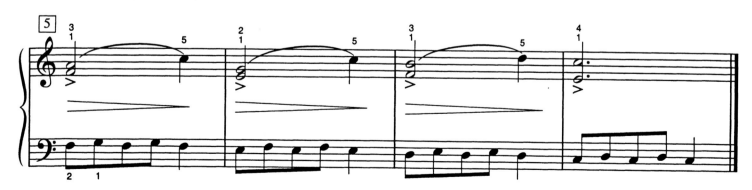

SCALE PASSAGES
right hand

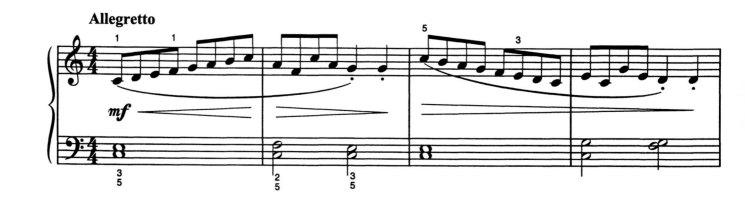

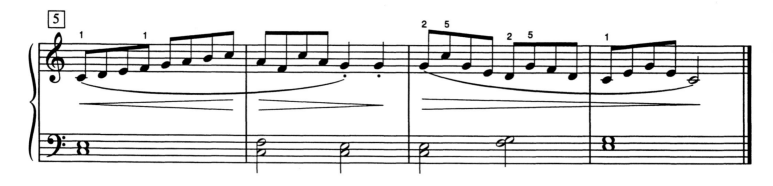

SCALE PASSAGES
left hand

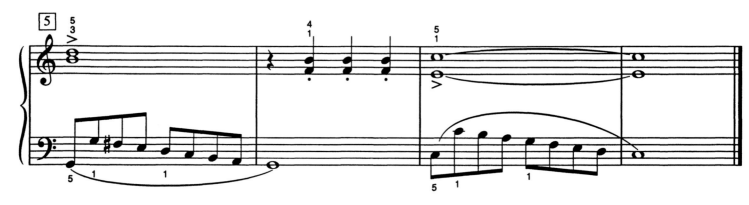

LEFT-HAND MELODY PLAYING

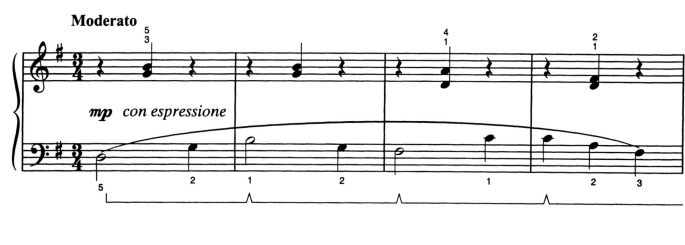

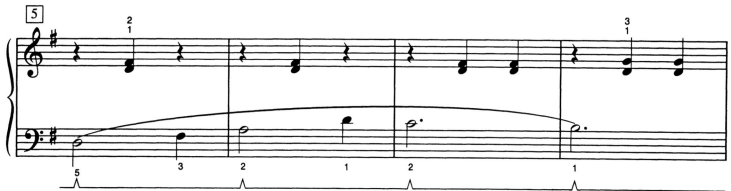

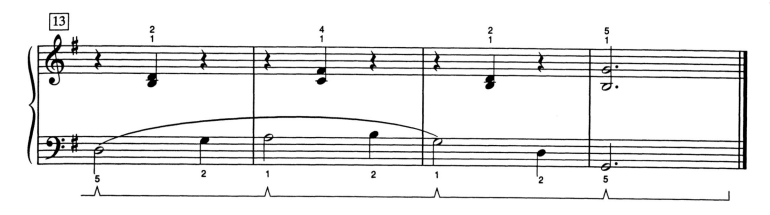

BROKEN CHORDS
right hand

BROKEN CHORDS
left hand

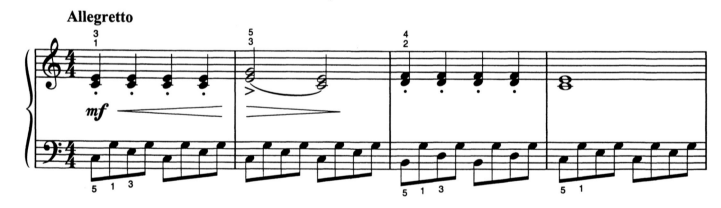

WRIST STACCATO

right hand

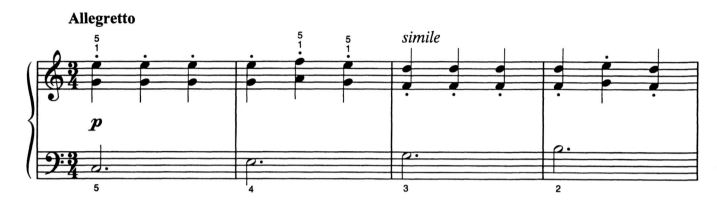

WRIST STACCATO
left hand

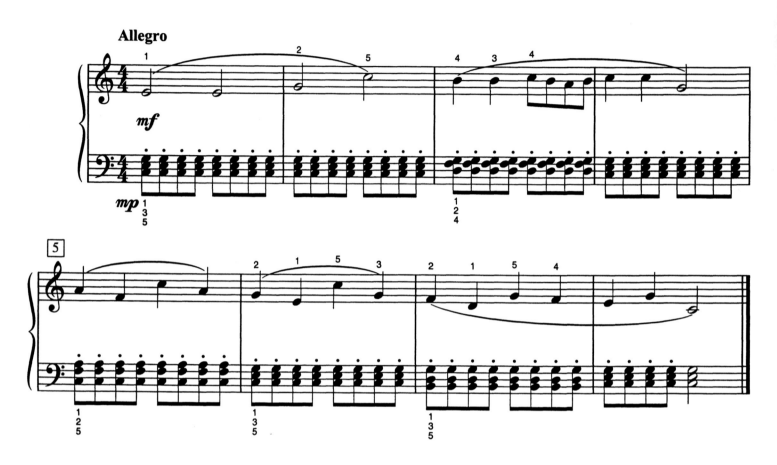

LEFT-HAND LEGATO STUDY

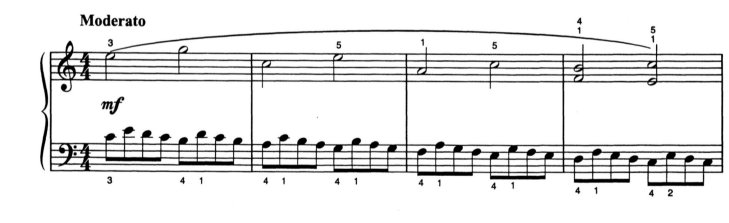

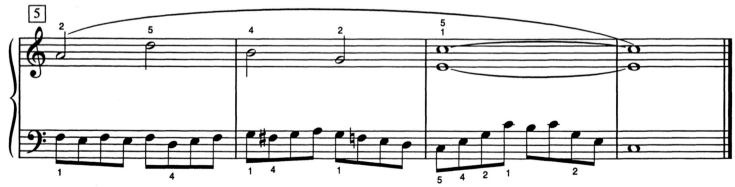

MELODY STUDY IN THIRDS

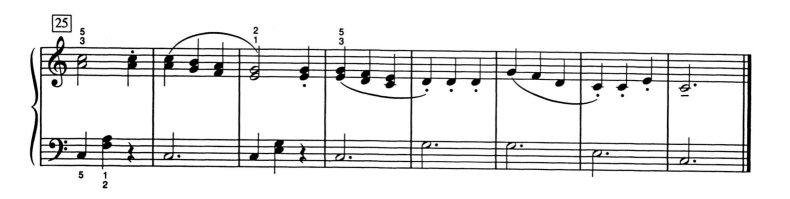

REPEATED NOTES

ACCOMPANIMENT PATTERN
left hand

RIGHT-HAND TURN TECHNIC

Tempo di valse

LEFT-HAND TURN TECHNIC

Allegro moderato

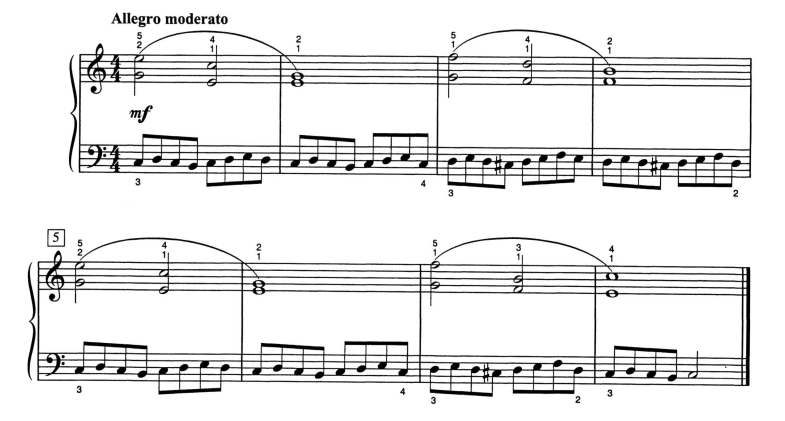

STUDY IN PHRASING

CHROMATIC CONTRACTIONS
right hand

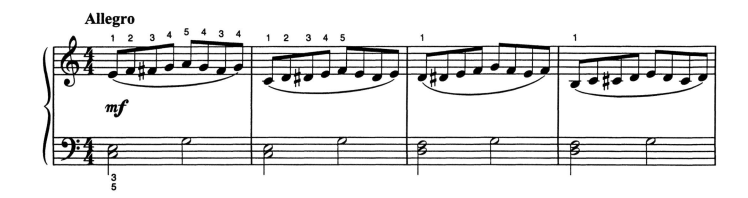

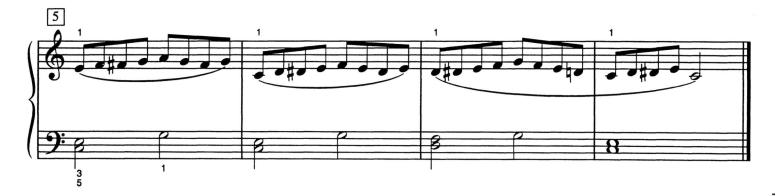

CHROMATIC CONTRACTIONS
left hand

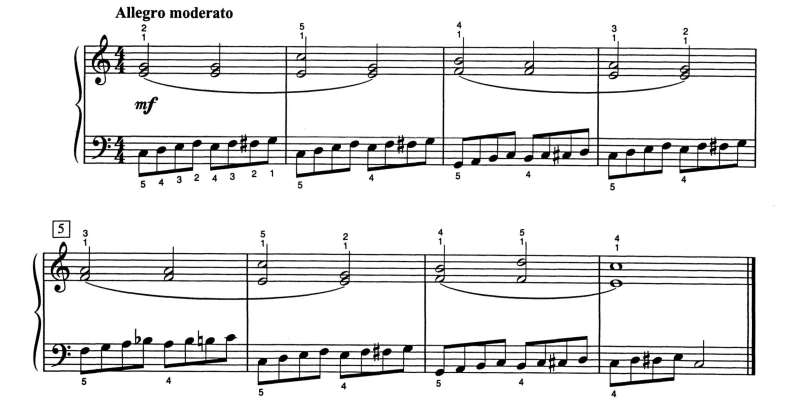

EL00285A

CHORD INVERSIONS

INTERWEAVING HAND LEGATO

BROKEN CHORDS
divided hands

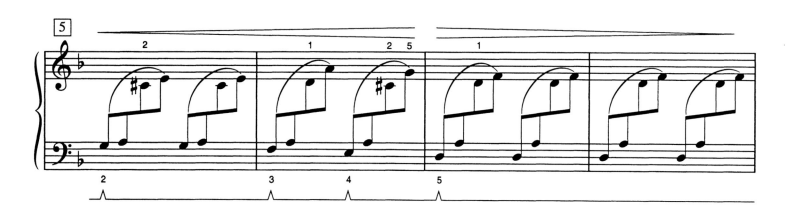

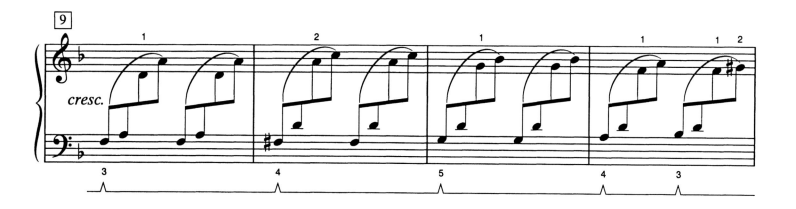

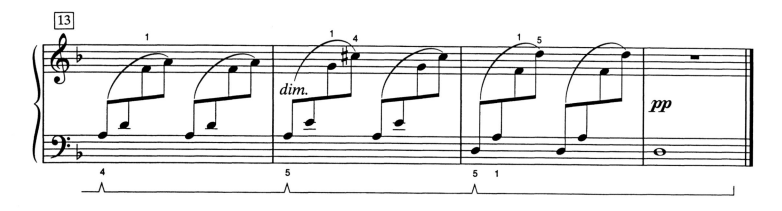

LEGATO AND STACCATO

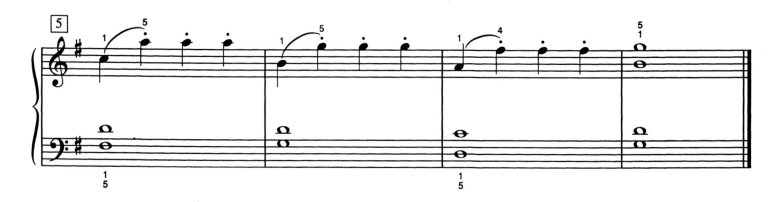

CROSSING HANDS STUDY

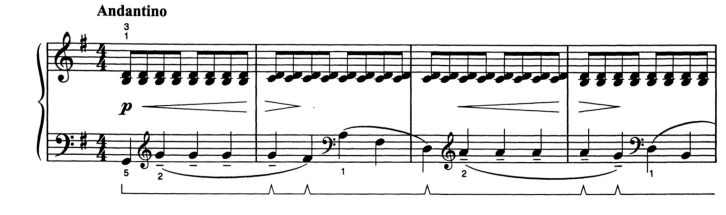

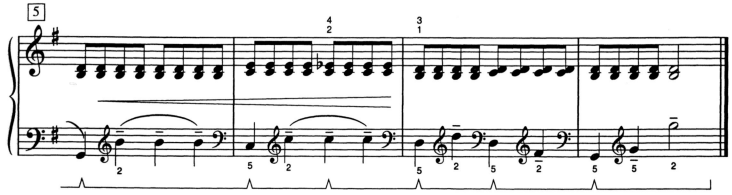

TRIPLET STUDY

ACCOMPANIMENT DESIGN

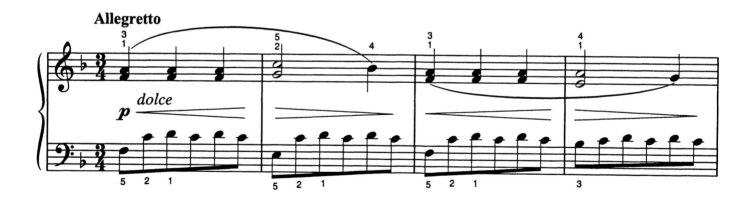

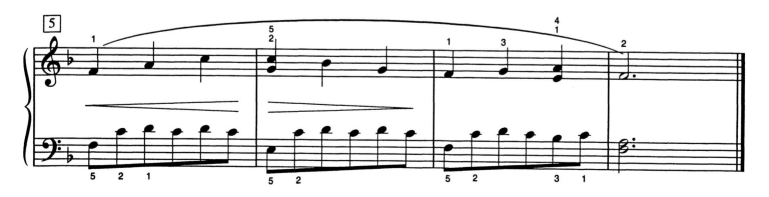

EL00285A

CONTINOUS SCALE PASSAGES

HOLDING TOP NOTES
right hand

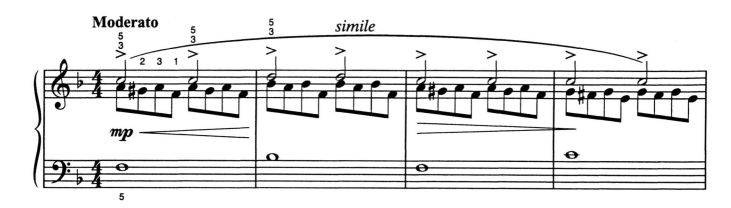

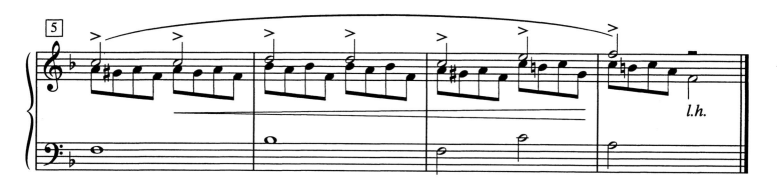

HOLDING BOTTOM NOTES
right hand

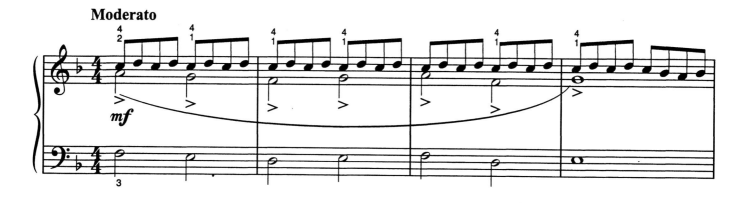

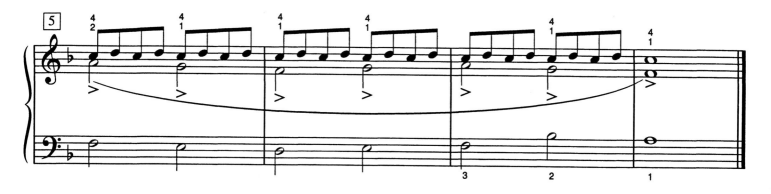

EL00285A

HOLDING TOP NOTES
left hand

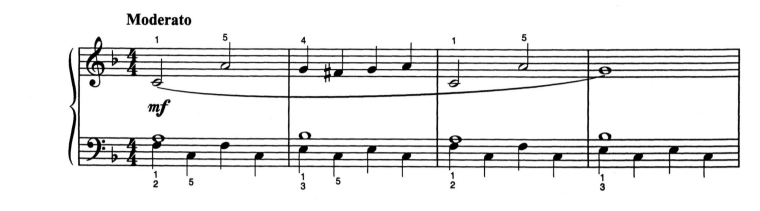

HOLDING BOTTOM NOTES
left hand

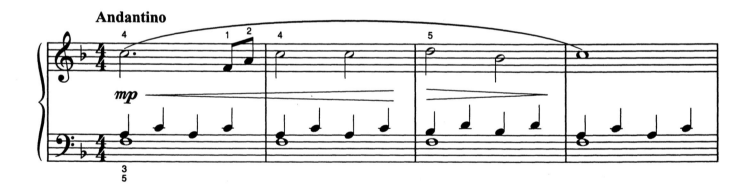

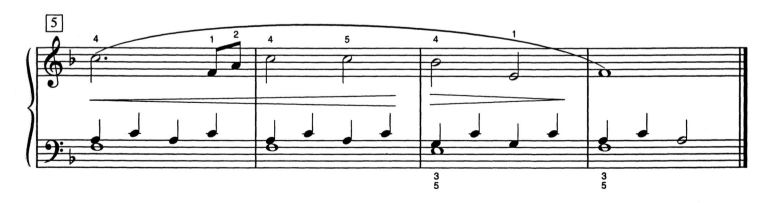

ACCOMPANIMENT IN TRIPLETS

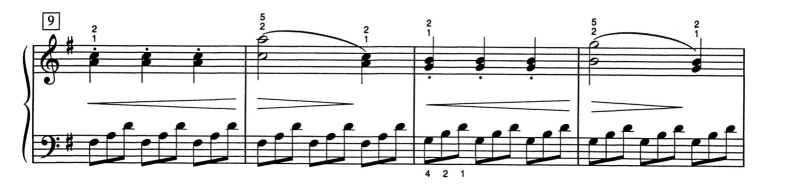

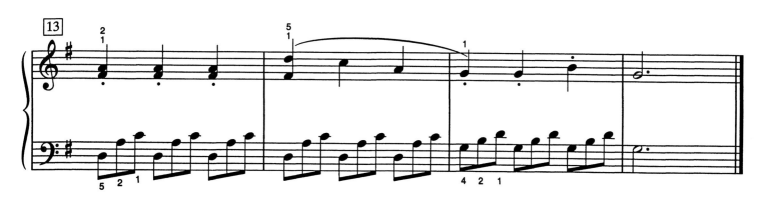

TWO NOTE SLURS

STRENGTHENING FINGERS 4 AND 5

ACCOMPANIMENT PATTERNS

with finger extensions

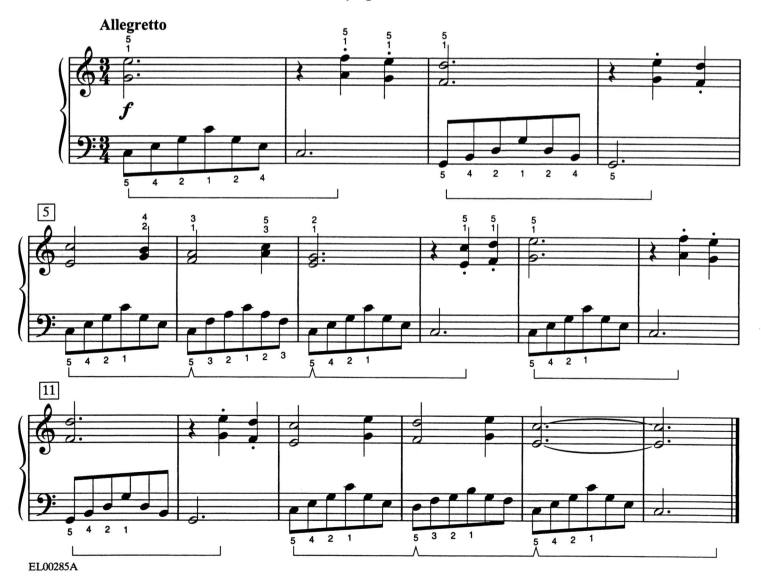

ACCOMPANIMENT IN THIRDS

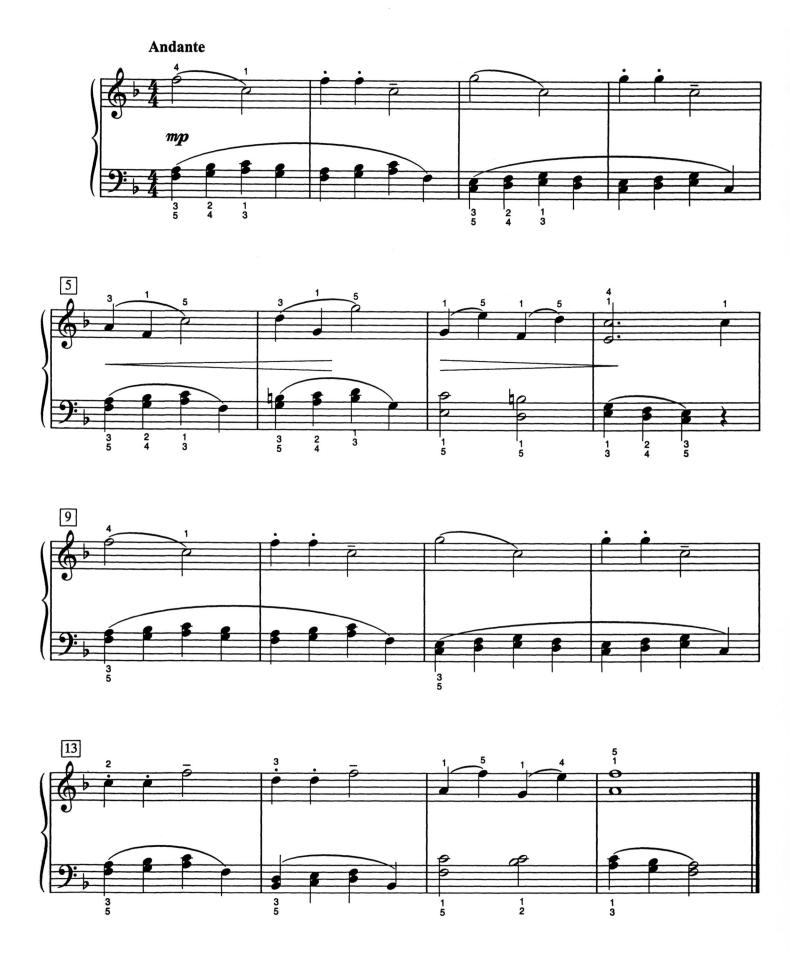

VELOCITY IN FIVE-FINGER GROUPS
right hand

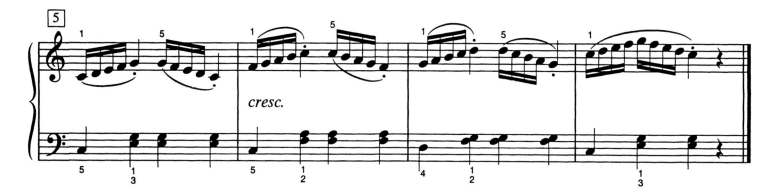

VELOCITY IN FIVE-FINGER GROUPS
left hand

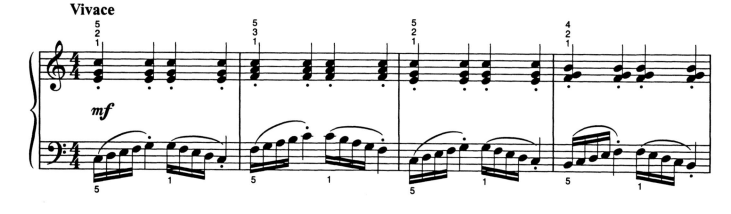

LEFT-HAND STACCATO MELODY

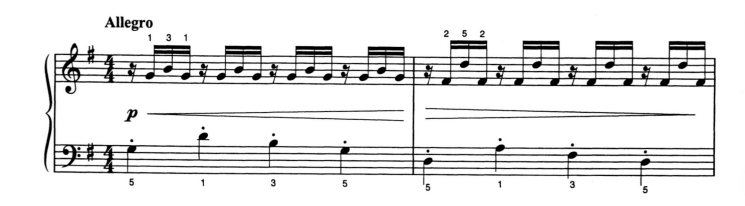

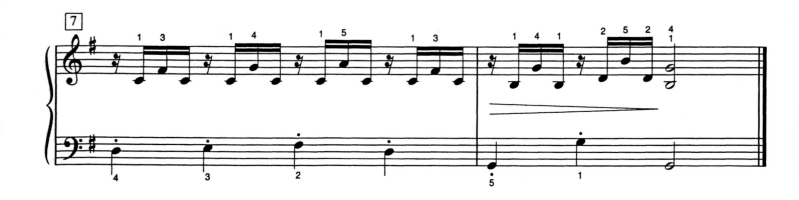